SECOND EDITION

Storybook 9

The
Orbit Book

by Sue Dickson

Illustrations by Norma Portadino, Jean Hamilton, Chip Neville and Kerstin Upmeyer

Printed in the United States of America

Copyright © 1998 Sue Dickson
International Learning Systems of North America, Inc.
Oldsmar, FL 34677

ISBN: 1-56704-519-7 (Volume 9)

D E F G H I J K L M N—CJK—05 04 03 02 01 00

Table of Contents
Raceway Step 22

2

A Fort for Kevin and Kate

Vocabulary

1. for
2. fort
3. forty
4. sort
5. torn
6. corn
7. store
8. order
9. pork
10. fork
11. forks
12. storm
13. short
14. cord
15. core
16. scorch
17. born
18. sore
19. sport
20. north
21. cork
22. thorn
23. shorts
24. organ
25. port
26. horn
27. form
28. stork
29. be fore
before

Story Words

30. wänt
31. to day
today
32. box
boxes
33. be gin
begin
34. too
35. near ly
nearly
36. plas tic
plastic
37. Mr.
(Mis ter)
38. in side
inside

3

Kevin said, "What can we do for fun?"

"We can make a fort for fun," said Kate.

"OK," said Kevin. "We will need some boxes. We must go to the store."

"Let's ask Mom if we may go," said Kate.

"Yes, you may go to the store," said Mom. "You can pick up my order. It is on this list. We need pork and corn and plastic forks for a picnic."

Kevin and Kate ran to the store. Kevin got Mom's order. Kate paid Mr. Gomez.

"Do you have any boxes?" asked Kate. "We need some."

"Yes," said Mr. Gomez, "but you will have to sort the boxes you want. They are in the back of the store. Many are wet and torn. We had a storm and some of the boxes got wet."

"Thank you !" said Kevin. "We will sort the boxes. We will not get a wet one or a torn one."

Kevin and Kate went to the back of the store.

"I see a box," yelled
Kate. "It has a big stork
on it."

"Here is a big apple
box," said Kevin. He
nearly fell in it!

9

"We picked the best boxes," said Kevin.

"We can fit the little boxes inside the big ones," said Kate.

"We can get Mom's order in, too !" said Kevin. "Let's go home so we can make our fort."

"We have seven boxes !" said Kevin. "What a fort we will have !"

"I am glad it is just a short way to North Street," said Kate.

11

"My legs will be sore before we get to North Street," said Kevin.

At last they got home! They gave Mom the order and ran to begin the fort.

See Kevin and Kate's fort ! What fun they will have ! Seven boxes make a fine big fort !

The End

Sheldon's Bike Crash

Vocabulary

1. Sheldon
2. hush
3. rush
4. crash
5. crush
6. dish
7. wish
8. polish

9. shin
10. shorts
11. shade
12. shall
13. sherbet
14. shake
15. shine
16. shoe (shoo)

Sheldon hopped up the street. He held his shin. He left his bike by the side of the street.

"What did you do ?" asked Sheldon's mom.

"I fell off my bike," said Sheldon. "My bike hit a stone and I flipped !

I was in a rush and I crashed !"

"Did you crush your hand ?" asked Mom.

"No, I just hit my shin and my shorts ripped," said Sheldon. "I wish I had not gone so fast !"

"Hush," said Mom. "I
wish you had not been
in a crash, too, Sheldon,
but you will be OK.
Come sit in the shade
and rest. I will get you
a Band-Aid."

18

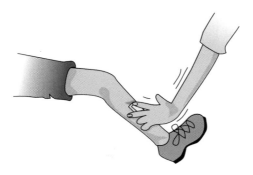

Mom stuck a Band-Aid on Sheldon's shin.

"Shall I get you a dish of sherbet?" she asked.

"Yes," said Sheldon. "Sherbet will be just grand."

When Mom came back,
Sheldon said, "See here,
Mom. What a mess ! My
shoe needs a Band-Aid,
too !"

"Shoe polish will fix that
and make it shine," said
Mom.

"Come eat your sherbet, Sheldon, and then **you** will shine !" said Mom.

Sheldon giggled. Mom was glad to see him happy once more.

The End

Cherry Hill Ranch

Vocabulary

1. each
2. bunch
3. lunch
4. bench
5. inch
6. munch
7. peach
8. beach
9. scorch
10. such
11. reach
12. hunch
13. church
14. march
15. torch
16. torches
17. cherry
18. children
19. cheese
20. chicken
21. chocolate
22. chase
23. Chucky
24. chapel
25. chime
26. chimes
27. teach
28. teacher
29. cheer
30. cheer ful cheerful
31. reaches
32. ranch

Story Word

(ŭ)
33. other

22

Each year a bunch of children go to Cherry Hill Ranch. The ranch is by a lake. The children swim in the lake.

Cherry Hill Ranch
LUNCH HUT

Each day the children eat
lunch in the Lunch Hut.
They sit on a bench.
Not one inch of the
bench is left to sit on !
The children munch on
cheese and chicken. They
have cherry punch. They
have peach pie or
chocolate cake.

24

After rest time, the children go to the beach. They chase each other across the sand to the lake.

"The hot sand will scorch your feet if you do not run fast !" yelled Chucky.

Such a race ! The kids cheer as each one reaches the lake !

Each one must pick a buddy to swim with. It is safe to swim when you have a buddy.

When the sun sets,
the sand is not so hot !
The children sit in a big
bunch on the beach.
The chapel chimes play
a tune. Such fun they
have !

A teacher reads them a story. The name of the story is "Three Cheers for Summer." It is such a cheerful story ! It makes all the children happy.

28

Next, the children march up the hill. Two children hold torches. The chapel bells chime. Off to bed they go at the end of the day.

Cherry Hill Ranch is such a cheerful place! I have a hunch the children will want to come back here each year!

The End

Vocabulary

1. each
2. teach
3. reach
4. torch
5. scorch
6. inch
7. much
8. porch
9. munch
10. chain
11. chisel
12. chip
13. chest
14. cherry
15. chose
16. champ
17. chunk
18. chocolate

Story Words

may be
19. maybe

care ful
20. careful

"I would like to make a hot rod," said Gus. "I would like to race it in the Hot Rod Race."

"Fine," said Dad. "I will help you make it."

31

Each day Dad and Gus did more.

Dad said, "We need a chain. Can you reach it, Gus ?"

"Yes, Dad," said Gus. "Will you need a torch, too ?"

"No," said Dad. "That will scorch it. A torch is just for metal."

"I need my chisel to chip off one inch from this end," said Dad. "You can reach it, Gus. It is in the chest."

"Yes, here it is," said Gus.

"I love my hot rod," said Gus. "Thank you, Dad. May I paint it today ? I would like to paint it red."

"I have some cherry red paint," said Dad. "See if you can reach it. It is on the shelf near the chest."

34

"I will teach you to paint," said Dad. "See me dip the brush in the can? I will press it on each side so the paint will not drip."

"I can do it," said Gus, "and it is fun! I will not spill or drip the paint. It is a little hot rod. It will not take much paint," he said.

Mom came in from the porch. "Such a fine hot rod ! I am glad you chose cherry red. Maybe you will be champ !" she said.

"I hope so, Mom," said Gus.

"It was a big job to
make a hot rod," said
Mom. "Here is a glass
of punch and a chunk of
chocolate to munch. Have
fun !"

"I will name my hot rod Red Flash. I will be a champ in my Red Flash. You must come to cheer the champ, Mom!" said Gus.

The End 39

A Shirt for a Third Grader

Vocabulary

1. term
2. teacher
3. Bert
4. her
5. over
6. clerk
7. stern
8. germs
9. fisher
10. big
    bigger
11. ever
12. grader
13. first
14. third
15. skirt
16. Shirley
17. shirt
18. girl
19. Thurs day
    Thursday

Story Word

20. sea shore
    seashore

The second grade term was over. Jenny waved good-by to her teacher.

Jenny and Shelly and Bert raced home.

"Mom! The term is over! I'm a third grader now!" yelled Jenny. "May we go to the seashore?" she asked.

"Yes, we will go next Thursday," said Mom. "Dad can come with us then."

"Yippee!" cried Jenny. "I love the seashore, but I need some bigger shorts and shirts."

"Fine," said Mom. "Let's go to the shop on Third Street."

Jenny and her mom went to the store to shop.

"I need a skirt," said Mom.

"I would like shorts and a shirt," said Jenny.

"We need a clerk," said Mom. "A clerk can help us."

A clerk came up to Jenny and her mom.

"I would like to try on the red shorts, the green ones, the gray ones and the yellow shirt," said Jenny.

"Wait, wait," said the clerk. She was very stern.

"You may not try on so many at one time. Take one or two, first. You may try on some more after."

Jenny went to try on the green shorts and the yellow shirt. "The green shorts are fine," said Jenny. "The yellow shirt is fine, too."

"You look nice," said Mom. "Here, try on the blue dotted shirt and the red shorts."

Buzz, buzz, buzz! A
big green fly buzzed in.

"Look at that fly!" said
Mom. "Get it, Jenny!
Do not let it get away!
It has germs!"

47

Jenny was ever so fast!
Swish !

"Good for me !" she said. "No more germs !"

"Fine," said Mom. "Let's try on the rest of your shorts."

Mom picked a pretty pink skirt. Jenny picked the green shorts and the yellow shirt.

"I will pay you," said Mom to the clerk.

"This shirt will be fun at the seashore," smiled Jenny. "I can't wait to go !"

The End

Chocolate Dirt

Vocabulary

1. Bert
2. jerk
3. thunder
4. germ
5. ever
   bet ter
6. better
7. Shirley
8. shirt
9. dirt
10. dirty
11. first
12. stir
13. firm
14. third
15. swirls
16. chirp
17. fir
18. hurt
19. curved
20. purple
21. turn

50

"Look ! The storm has ended," said Shirley. "The thunder and rain have stopped. Let's go, Bert. We can make some mud pies !"

"I have an old shirt on," said Bert. "I can get it dirty. Let's make a chocolate cake."

"OK," said Shirley.

"First, we must fill up my purple pail with dirt and stir it," said Shirley.

"Second, we must pack it till it is firm."

53

"Third, we will turn it over and lift up the pail," said Shirley.

"Try not to jerk it or it will spill," said Bert.

"Here, Bert. You may make the swirls on top. Use the curved stick to make swirls," said Shirley.

"Look," said Bert. "I see a bird. Did you hear it chirp in our fir tree? He is asking if our cake is real."

Shirley giggled. "We cannot let him eat it. He may get a germ ! It would hurt his tummy !"

"No sir, a bird will not be tricked by our mud pies," said Bert. "He is not so silly !"

"My tummy tells me it is lunch time," said Bert. "I like chocolate dirt, but Mom's real cake is better! Let's go in for lunch... and Mom's cake! I'll race you, Shirley!"

The winner gets the biggest slice!

And off they went!

Have **you** ever made a chocolate dirt cake?

The End

57

Chipper Gets Hurt

Vocabulary

1. Curly

2. urge

3. burst

4. turn

5. hurt

6. burn

7. hurry

8. curl

9. curb

10. Kurt

Story Words

vis it
11. visit

on to
12. onto

in to
13. into

14. then

15. love (luv)

any more
16. anymore

58

Chipper was a little black dog. He did not like to stay at home. He had the urge to run away. So one day he did !

On his way he met a big dog. The big dog had brown and white fur. His tail had a big curl in it.

"May I run away with you?" asked Chipper.

"Yes," said the big dog.

"You may come with me. My name is Curly. We will go visit my dog pals."

"Let's turn onto North Street," said Curly.

Just then some children shot a rocket into the sky.

"Look!" they yelled. "Run fast so you will not get hurt! It may burst!"

Chipper ran but the
rocket fell by him.

He did not want it to
hurt him.

He jumped up on the
curb and fell.

"Curly ! Curly !" he yelled. "I cannot run away. I have hurt my leg."

"I will go home," said Chipper. "My master, Kurt, will fix me up. He will take care of me. He loves me. I do not have the urge to run away anymore."

63

Chipper ran home to
Kurt in a hurry!
The End